The Zoo's Who's Who

Sea Lions

Katie Franks

PowerKiDS press.
New York

Published in 2015 by The Rosen Publishing Group, Inc.
29 East 21st Street, New York, NY 10010

First Edition

Editor: Jennifer Way
Photo Research: Katie Stryker
Book Design: Joe Carney

Photo Credits: Cover Cloudia Newland/iStock/Thinkstock; p. 5 Andreas Neßlinger/iStock/Thinkstock; p. 6 bbourdages/iStock/Thinkstock; p. 9 Image Source/Getty Images; p. 10 Teresa Gueck/iStock/Thinkstock; p. 13 NatalieJean/Shutterstock.com; p. 14 Steve Estvanik/Shutterstock.com; pp. 17, 21 John Foxx/Stockbyte/Thinkstock; p. 18 MichaelStubblefield/iStock/Thinkstock; p. 22 Irina Lemberskaya/iStock/Thinkstock; p. 24 AlexGoldblum/iStock/Thinkstock.

Library of Congress Cataloging-in-Publication Data

Franks, Katie, author.
Sea lions / by Katie Franks. — First edition.
pages cm. — (The zoo's who's who)
Includes index.
ISBN 978-1-4777-6473-2 (library binding) — ISBN 978-1-4777-6585-2 (pbk.) —
ISBN 978-1-4777-6586-9 (6-pack)
1. Sea lions—Juvenile literature. 2. Zoo animals—Juvenile literature. I. Title.
QL737.P63F73 2015
599.79'75—dc23

2013048492

Manufactured in the United States of America

CPSIA Compliance Information: Batch #WS14PK4: For Further Information contact Rosen Publishing, New York, New York at 1-800-237-9932

Contents

Sea lions are furry animals with **flippers**. They live along coasts of oceans and seas all over the world.

Can you tell a sea lion from a seal? Look at the ears. Sea lions have **ear flaps**. Seals do not.

California sea lions live along the west coast of North America. They eat mostly fish, squid, and clams.

There are seven kinds of sea lions. Steller sea lions are the largest kind.

Sea lions are good swimmers. They dive underwater. Some sea lions can stay underwater for up to 9 minutes!

Sea lions talk to each other by barking. They can be very noisy!

Sea lions form a large group called a **colony**. They do this when they have babies.

A baby sea lion is a **pup**. Females have one pup at a time.

Galápagos sea lion mothers care for their pups for up to three years. Then the pup is an adult.

It is fun to watch sea lions swim and play!

WORDS TO KNOW

colony

ear flap

flipper

pup

WEBSITES

Due to the changing nature of Internet links, PowerKids Press has developed an online list of websites related to the subject of this book. This site is updated regularly. Please use this link to access the list: www.powerkidslinks.com/zww/sea/

INDEX